FOREWORD

The Civil Service Club in Great Scotland Yard is a un
building at the historic heart of government in Whitehall. U¡ ....une
in 1952, Her Majesty The Queen made the premises ava.. ... . Club to provide 'a
social facility within the reach of all.' Today the Club is thriving as never before, with more
than 12,000 members and a mission true to its original founding. Enjoy the tale and come
to visit us again soon.

Sir Peter Housden, KCB

Chair, Civil Service Club

The Origins of the Civil Service Club

The origins of the Civil Service Club may be found in the evolution of organised sport. On 4 November 1921 a meeting was held in the George Thomas Room at Methodist Central Hall, Westminster to consider a proposition for the formation of a Civil Service Sports Council (CSSC) to function as an umbrella body for the many sporting bodies in the Home Civil Service. More than 50 clubs and associations, including the Civil Service Athletics Association and the Civil Service Football Club, were represented. The meeting was chaired by Sir Aubrey Vere Symonds, Second Permanent Secretary at the Ministry of Health, who moved the proposition, which was unanimously carried by those present.

In early 1922 the proposed body received the blessing of Sir Warren Fisher, Permanent Secretary of HM Treasury and Head of the Home Civil Service. Sir Aubrey was elected CSSC Chairman and Sir Noel Curtis-Bennett, Divisional Inspector at the Ministry of Health, initially became Honorary Treasurer. Within a few months the Duke of York (later King George VI) agreed to become President and, in 1923, King George V consented to become Patron. At this distance of time we can certainly consider Curtis-Bennett to have been the nation's first professional sports administrator. He would serve as CSSC Vice-Chairman for more than 20 years, eventually becoming its Chairman in 1942. David Goldblatt in his 2016 book *The Games: A Global History of the Olympics* would describe Curtis-Bennett as: 'a man of such maniacal sporting and bureaucratic zeal that, at one point, he held official posts in over 60 sporting organisations and would die of a stroke while addressing the West Ham Boys and Amateur Boxing Club in 1950.'

Sport has traditionally played an important role in British culture and has given birth to a range of major international sports. In the earliest days of British organised sport the Civil Service provided many of the top-class sportsmen and women of the period and, inevitably, Civil Service teams and clubs would be the founders or instigators of a number of sporting bodies. Indeed, on 26 October 1863, eleven amateur football clubs met at the Freemasons' Tavern on London's Great Queen Street to found the English Football Association. Only one of those clubs survives to this day - the Civil Service Football Club, represented on that occasion by Mr George Twizell Wawn from West Bolden in County Durham, a Clerk 3rd Class at the War Office in Pall Mall and a stout defender on the pitch.

War came again on 3 September 1939. More than three million people were evacuated from Britain's major cities, some 15 million ration books were delivered, thousands of temporary civil servants were engaged and a handful of new government departments prepared themselves for the challenge of organising life on the 'Home Front'.

During that conflict the CSSC undertook the provision of sports facilities at the out-stations, to which many civil servants had been dispersed. The success of the centres run by the CSSC led, in 1943, to it revising its own rules to permit the provision of recreational and social facilities. On 28 March 1944 at London's National Portrait Gallery, off Trafalgar Square, the CSSC commenced its Annual General Meeting. Mr H G Poor moved a resolution which stated: 'This Annual General Meeting of the Civil Service Sports Council Ltd instructs its Executive Council to appoint a sub-committee for the purpose of exploring the possibility of acquiring suitable premises in London to be used as a Civil Service Sports and Social Club, the cost to be met by money raised through the formation of a limited liability company inviting only civil servants to subscribe for £1 shares if necessary, such a club to be subsidised by the Civil Service Sports Council Limited'.

The Royal Nuptials

After much discussion the resolution was carried without dissent. A sub-committee would be established under Mr F A Hartman's chairmanship to explore the possibility of acquiring premises in London. Similar resolutions were passed with increasing support at successive CSSC AGMs. At the height of the Second World War the government was busy contending with the challenges arising from the need to harness the nation's manpower and economic strength to one sole purpose - the defeat of the Axis Powers.

For that reason alone, every building likely to be suitable as a social centre had already been requisitioned by the Ministry of Works. Added to which the CSSC's resources were, at that point, fully committed to meeting its liabilities in respect of the maintenance and upkeep of grounds and sports facilities at evacuation centres. The CSSC thus found itself without the financial means to carry its plans into effect, even if it had identified a suitable property. On the evening of 7 May 1945 Britons learned from BBC Radio that the conflict in Europe was over. That news was received with relief by a grateful nation and Japan surrendered on 15 August. The government commenced dismantling the machinery of war and restoring the nation's fabric, although food rationing would not end until 4 July 1954. It would take the return of peace to remove the obstacles to the CSSC's plans. The Princess Elizabeth first encountered Philip, Prince of Greece at the wedding of Princess Marina of Greece and Denmark and Prince George, Duke of Kent in 1934. After a third meeting in July 1939 the future Queen, who was just 13 years old at the time, is said to have fallen in love with Philip and they began exchanging letters.

The couple became secretly engaged in 1946 and Elizabeth's father, King George VI, ordered that any formal engagement was delayed until after his daughter's 21st birthday in April 1947. The engagement was officially announced in July that same year.

In advance of the wedding of the Princess Elizabeth and Lieutenant Philip Mountbatten, RN, Duke of Edinburgh, which took place on 20 November 1947 at Westminster Abbey, the Home Civil Service and Foreign Service undertook a collection for the purpose of purchasing a suitable present to celebrate the royal nuptials. Two silver salvers were purchased from silversmith C J Vander of Fetter Lane, London.

The gifts are in the Royal Collection, being catalogued RCIN 15971 and RCIN 15972. The first is a circular silver salver in George II style, with moulded rim, on four scroll feet, the centre engraved with the coat of arms of the Duke of Edinburgh, with crest and supporters. Engraved on the reverse is the inscription: 'A gift / on their marriage / to Her Royal Highness / The Princess Elizabeth and / Lieutenant Philip Mountbatten RN / from all ranks of / His Majesty's Civil and / Foreign Services / 20 November 1947.' The second is also a circular silver salver in George II style, with moulded rim, on four scroll feet, the centre engraved with the coat of arms of the Princess Elizabeth, with coronet and supporters. Engraved on the reverse is the inscription: 'A gift / on their marriage / to Her Royal Highness / The Princess Elizabeth and / Lieutenant Philip Mountbatten RN / from all ranks of / His Majesty's Civil and / Foreign Services / 20 November 1947.'

The couple received more than 2,500 wedding presents from around the world, which were displayed in an exhibition mounted at St James's Palace, which attracted more than 200,000 visitors. The accompanying brochure described Gift 1118 as: 'HIS MAJESTY'S CIVIL AND FOREIGN SERVICES / Pair of large silver salvers of plain design with Bath / borders and scroll feet.'

The Two Silver Salvers

The Prince Philip Salver - Royal Collection Trust / All Rights Reserved.

The Princess Elizabeth Salver - Royal Collection Trust / All Rights Reserved.

The Queen's Gift

The balance of the Wedding Fund collected by the Home Civil Service and the Foreign Service was £14,037 (equivalent to £539,525.94 in 2018). The Princess Elizabeth was touched by the kindness of the gesture and made her wish known that the balance should be handed over to the CSSC, with the express intention that it be utilised to establish a social facility for civil servants: 'on condition that membership should be available to all grades and classes at a subscription within reach of all.' In time, that remarkable instance of royal generosity would become known to all concerned as 'The Queen's Gift.'

As post-war Britain slowly returned to normality, the best minds of the Senior Civil Service redoubled their efforts to identify a suitable premises in the neighbourhood. They soon noticed the purpose-built fire house at 13-15 Great Scotland Yard, which was scheduled to become vacant in the early part of 1953, when it would cease to function as a press bureau for the Festival of Britain and was due to be handed back to the Ministry of Works. The Queen's Gift would enable the CSSC to bring its plan for a Civil Service Club to fruition, with a substantial sum in reserve, should they be minded to draw upon it.

On 6 February 1952 King George VI died in his sleep at Sandringham in Norfolk and the Princess Elizabeth, who was then overseas on a royal tour of Kenya, acceded to the throne as Queen Elizabeth II. Upon her return to England, Her Majesty would write: 'On my accession to the Throne, I desire to convey my warm thanks to all grades of the Civil Service for the able and devoted manner in which they have carried out their duties during the reign of my father. The high respect in which the Civil Service is held in the United Kingdom is the reward of centuries of faithful work for the community. Its traditions and standards are shared by the younger Civil Services of the countries of the Commonwealth. I know that the loyal and steadfast spirit of all of these services will be my enduring support throughout whatever difficulties the future may hold in store.'

On 11 December 1952 Sir Edward Bridges, Permanent Secretary to HM Treasury and Head of the Home Civil Service, wrote to all government departments informing them that a Civil Service Club would soon be opening in Whitehall and seeking the support of the workforce for that worthy enterprise. In his covering note Sir Edward exhorted their permanent secretaries to do all they could personally to ensure the success of the scheme. (The full text of his circular may be found at Annex A). Former Ministry of Labour permanent secretary Sir Godfrey Ince, Chairman of the CSSC, added his voice to that of Sir Edward, thus ensuring that his council members, area associations and affiliated bodies were kept fully in the picture. Unsurprisingly, given the many years he had devoted to the project, Mr F A Hartman would be appointed the club's first chairman. (A comprehensive list of chairmen may be found at Annex G). Mr Charles F Stewart was appointed the club's honorary secretary on secondment from HM Treasury. Given the workload involved from the outset, he undertook the role full-time and, upon retirement at the end of 1953, was taken on by the club as a member of staff. The club's officers entered into negotiations with the Ministry of Works to obtain a lease on the premises and a bank account was opened with Holt's Branch of the private bank Glyn, Mills & Company, a stone's throw away at 22 Whitehall (later the Civil Service Commission and, currently, the headquarters of the Department for International Development). Thus the Civil Service Club in Great Scotland Yard was brought into being as a social centre for all civil servants, both serving and retired, whether resident in London, or in the provinces.

The Young Queen

Her Majesty Queen Elizabeth II, photographed at the commencement of her reign.

The Club's Management Committee

Sir Edward Bridges firmly resisted the notion that the premises should be licensed to sell alcoholic beverages. He only gave way under the pressure of popular demand and an application for a license to sell alcohol was submitted to the Board of Green Cloth at St James's Palace. In a throwback to Great Scotland Yard's historic origins, the club came under the jurisdiction of that royal body, which was presided over by the Lord Steward.

It audited the accounts of the Royal Household and undertook arrangements for royal travel. It also sat as a court upon offences committed within the verge of the royal palaces. Its jurisdiction was limited to the sale of alcohol, betting and gaming licenses for premises falling within the areas attached to, or governed by, the royal palaces. There were a number of public houses and clubs within the jurisdiction of the board, which was limited to what had been the private grounds of the sovereign and they included Carlton House Terrace, the northern end of Whitehall and the National Gallery (former site of the Royal Mews). With the reforms to local government licensing brought about by the 2003 Licensing Act, the Board of Green Cloth would disappear into the pages of history

Without fanfare, the club opened its doors for business on the morning of 2 February 1953. The *Civil Service Sports Journal* reported in their edition of March 1953: 'It was a bit of a scramble to get everything ready for the opening, but somehow, it was done and the doors were opened on 2 February as had been announced. Contrary to expectations there was a fairly gentle flow of visitors. Everyone was thrilled with the style and furnishing of the club and the few that had any criticism did no more than express doubts about the premises being large enough. I said in my notes last month that voluntary workers had managed to cope with the rush of applications. I spoke too soon! Since that time, the increasing band of helpers has been overwhelmed by a deluge of forms. I understand that the lost ground is being made up and that those who were disturbed about the late receipt of membership cards will soon be receiving them.'

The club's Management Committee comprised twelve members and was originally a sub-committee of the CSSC, until the year following when the membership elected their own officers for a three-year term at AGM. The officers of the club comprised a chairman, vice-chairman, honorary secretary and treasurer, who were all initially appointed by the CSSC from among the club's membership. The long process of the club unwinding and redefining its relationship with the CSSC would take more than 60 years and was only completed by changes to the club's constitution enacted in 2018.

The inaugural meeting of the club's Management Committee duly took place on the evening of 24 February. On the first agenda was the intense disdain of the two hall porters for the second-hand uniforms they had been allocated and planning for the celebrations of the impending coronation of Queen Elizabeth II at Westminster Abbey on 2 June 1953. In time-honoured Civil Service fashion, much of the day-to-day administration of the club would be devolved to sub-committees established for specific purposes. Indeed, such was the enthusiasm for establishing and serving on sub-committees, one was even convened to mastermind and supervise the decoration of the Tea Bar. By far and away the greatest burden fell on the shoulders of the enthusiastic catering sub-committee, which spent much of the early years grappling with prices, mechanical ovens, portion control, the drawing up of menus, the procurement of catering equipment, staff shortages and the never-ending quest for a suitable catering manager.

The First Year of the Club's Existence

In the first year of the club's existence, the minutes of the Management Committee disclose that they considered such knotty issues as: staff wages, cloakroom insurance, tipping in the restaurant, lift problems, dilapidations, beer temperature, smoking at the tea counter, the proposed establishment of a barbers' shop, the consternation caused by the constant disappearance of magazines from the lounges, the size and cost of pats of butter, soft furnishing issues, stocktakes and the enduring saga of the missing teaspoons - a hardy perennial, which would feature on the committee's agenda for decades.

     In the early days a number of hall porters were discharged from the club's service, having been found unfit for duty through drink, usually having been purchased by well-meaning members. The management took pains to take up references and make discreet enquiries into the background, habits and religious affiliations of potential hall porters but, in time, would learn through bitter experience that the more godly and upright the candidate for the post was held to be, the more likely it was that he would be corrupted by the members, who would insist on demonstrating their generosity. Both committee and club management would eventually learn that worldly men were less likely to succumb to temptation. In the fullness of time, the committee recognised that ex-servicemen tended to be the steadiest and most reliable types.

Civil servants taking a break from their labours in the club's bar in the 1970s.

The Club's Membership

The election of proposed members took place in committee, with batches of names being presented for approval, these being proposed and seconded by officers nominated for the purpose. Each successful applicant would, in due course, be sent a membership card in a black cover, which bore the title 'Civil Service Club' in gilt lettering.

However, the rate at which civil servants applied for membership of the club caused serious administrative problems for the staff. At one point applications were arriving much faster than they could be processed and that development caught the Management Committee wholly unprepared. Its officers would be haunted for years by the question of what would happen if all these members turned up on the premises at the same time. For that reason, the committee called a halt to all enrolments when the membership figure arrived at 27,000. Following that decision, a waiting list was compiled of all subsequent applications. After monitoring the situation for some months, the committee decided to lift the embargo in the knowledge that bringing the top three floors of the premises into service would help to cope with any additional usage arising from increased membership. The matter was then kept under constant review by the committee until it settled down. The club's earliest membership records disclose that, at the outset, the elected membership of the club was 17,895 members, which quickly rose to 24,825 by the end of March 1953. By June of that year there were 29,657 members.

On 31 December 1953 there were 31,972 members. These being 130 Associate Members, 13,061 Country Members and 18,601 Town Members, who paid a subscription of a penny a week, deducted from salary. In the early months the committee spent much time debating the intent behind the club's Rule Four, which determined which civil servants, of which departments, could become members. They assessed the eligibility for membership of the staff of organisations such as Trinity House, the British Electricity Authority and the Medical Research Council. Those New Scotland Yard civil servants who had been erroneously admitted to the club's membership were speedily refunded.

One particular organisation which fell foul of Rule Four was the Crown Agents' Office, whose staff were servants of the Crown but not part of the Home Civil Service. Despite some fairly heavy artillery being wheeled onto the battlefield, the Management Committee refused to budge from their position that these staff were not civil servants and thus ineligible for membership. That situation was complicated by the fact that the CSSC constantly reviewed and revised its own criteria as to what constituted a 'fringe body'. By the mid-1960s the club was shedding some 500 members a year, which ensured that this potential source of new members would remain a permanent fixture on the Management Committee's agenda. Motions attempting to amend Rule Four would dominate the agenda of the club's early AGMs and these proposed to broaden the interpretation of the rule to include staff of the Church Commission for England, the Crown Agents, the Overseas Audit Service, the Imperial War Graves Commission and others. The staff of all of these organisations would in time, become eligible for membership.

For the first half century of its existence, club AGMs were well-attended affairs, usually being held on the premises of a nearby government department as the club was not nearly large enough to hold all those who wished to attend in person. Such proceedings would be enlivened by unscripted contributions and interventions from the floor, which was dreaded by some of the club's officers, but kept them all on their toes.

The Royal Visit

The civil servants who comprised the original Management Committee kept a close eye on the day-to-day running of the club, asked searching questions on the right issues, were fortunate in their selection of key personnel and quickly acquired a degree of commercial awareness. Consequently, the club quickly achieved a healthy trading surplus.

The minutes of the Management Committee meeting held at the club on the evening of 11 May 1953 detail the feverish planning underway in preparation for the queen's coronation at Westminster Abbey on 2 June 1953 and an application for a late license was duly submitted to the Board of Green Cloth. The coronation date was chosen specifically on the advice of experts at the Meteorological Office, who predicted that it was statistically likely to have the best weather. Unfortunately, the day would be overcast, with sporadic outbreaks of rain and a chill wind. General Manager Mr Bendall would report to the Management Committee: 'enquiries had been received from the staff as to additional remuneration for Coronation Day. He reported that he had informed them that, in addition to the appropriate pay for the day, some extra allowance or bonus would be made: This would depend upon the services performed and the *zeal* of those concerned.'

In the early years the social highlight of the club's year was the Annual Dinner and Dance, usually held at a hotel in London's West End. In those heady days attendance was limited to 600 guests and tickets were available at the price of two guineas each. On such occasions evening dress was the order of the day, for both ladies and gentlemen.

On the first such occasion, held at the Dorchester Hotel on Park Lane on the evening of 2 February 1954, Chancellor of the Exchequer 'Rab' Butler was guest of honour. He had an exceptionally long ministerial career and was one of only two British politicians (the other being John Simon, 1st Viscount Simon) to have served in three of the four great offices of state, but never to have become prime minister, for which Butler was passed over in 1957 and 1963. He delivered an address lauding the club's objectives and achievements in the most generous terms. During his peroration he stated: 'A civil servant does not regard himself as belonging to some self-contained section that works in Whitehall, or in a country town, or overseas. He belongs to the general body and makes his own particular contribution to its work.' Mr Butler's speech concluded with the line: 'This is a very happy enterprise. I hope that it will go on from strength to strength.'

Sir Edward Bridges wrote to Lieutenant Colonel Sir Michael Adeane, the Queen's Private Secretary at Buckingham Palace, to arrange an official visit by The Queen for the purpose of a formal opening of the establishment and, as is usual for such events, much detailed planning went into the royal visit, which took place at Remembrancetide on 10 November 1954. Sir Michael made it known to the officers of the Management Committee that Her Majesty wanted to see the club functioning, just as it would on any ordinary day, and that she would be pleased to partake of a glass of sherry immediately prior to her departure. Lieutenant Colonel Martin Charteris, the Queen's Assistant Private Secretary, would subsequently write to inform the officers of the Management Committee: 'How greatly the Queen had enjoyed her visit and how impressed she was with all that she saw. Her Majesty was delighted to see that the Wedding Fund had been put to such good purpose and further commanded Colonel Charteris to thank the committee very much for the refreshment given her at the end of the visit.' At that time, Her Majesty graciously consented to become Patron of the Civil Service Club and remains so to the present day.

The Early Years

The architect Hilton Wright was engaged to bring the fourth and fifth floors of the premises into commission as overnight accommodation for members and the necessary building work was quickly set in hand. Mr Wright was no stranger to 13-15 Great Scotland Yard, having previously been responsible for converting the premises into a press bureau in readiness for the Festival of Britain. His endeavours would be rewarded by the Management Committee with life membership of the club, the very first grant of its kind.

The first outing to the Derby at Epsom Downs Racecourse in Surrey took place in the club's very first year of business, with tickets going on sale to members at a price of 32 shillings and sixpence. That bibulous, coach-borne jamboree on the first Saturday of June has been a staple feature of the club's social calendar ever since.

The concrete reinforced air raid shelters, which had been installed under the building during the late war, quickly proved unsuitable for keeping wine, a problem soon resolved by Mr Hurst, the consulting architect, who quickly arranged for the installation of ventilation in order to maintain a constant temperature in the cellar. In 1959, through the agency of the Ministry of Works, the building was connected to the 'Whitehall District Heating Scheme', otherwise known as 'The Grid', which supplied heating from furnaces in the basement of the nearby Whitehall Gardens Building, which housed the Air Ministry and the Board of Trade (today, the Ministry of Defence). The Grid would produce its own unique challenges in the decades following. For that reason, in or out of the public realm, the premises continued to be maintained by the Ministry of Works and, following its demise in 1970, by the Property Services Agency and its successor, BM South East.

In due course, complaints from members would be lodged with the Management Committee, each one having to be investigated and pondered at length. Conversely, disciplinary issues would also arise from the conduct of the membership, with individuals being held to account for the non-removal of headgear by gentlemen in the bar, along with instances of poor behaviour in the club and cheques being returned by the bank marked 'refer to drawer.' It says much about how British society's attitude to disability has changed since 1960 that a club member (who worked for the Board of Trade) had to write to the Management Committee to request permission for her guide dog to access the premises. The committee agreed (a) to the admission of the guide dog in question, on the understanding that it would be kept under control, and (b) to a continuance of the discretion vested in the club secretary or manager in any future similar case.

On 11 February 1966 the club held its Annual Dinner and Dance at the Europa Hotel on Mayfair's Park Lane. Club President Sir Laurence Helsby received the guests. The guest of honour on that occasion was Douglas Houghton, MP, Chancellor of the Duchy of Lancaster. Over a span of 38 years, from 1922 to 1960, Houghton was General Secretary of the Inland Revenue Staff Federation. Under his leadership that trade union attracted a 95 per cent voluntary membership, without the benefit of a 'closed shop', despite the fact that its 10,000 members were scattered across some 600 towns and offices the length and breadth of the UK. The top table that night included: Sir Charles Cunningham, KCB, KBE, CVO (Home Office); Sir John Winnifrith, KCB (Ministry of Agriculture, Fisheries and Food); Sir Henry Hardman, KCB (Ministry of Defence); Sir Harvey Druitt, KCB (Chairman of the Civil Service Sports Council) and Mr Richard Hayward (Secretary General, Civil Service National Whitley Council (Staff Side)).

The Epsom Derby

Someone rather important arriving on the course.

Club Members assessing the generosity of the on-course bookies.

The Naming of Rooms and Lounges

The 1 November 1966 minutes of the Management Committee record: 'The Secretary said that, following on the authorisation given at the last Committee Meeting, he had again interviewed Mr Harkins with the result that, on 10 October 1966, he had taken up the appointment of Catering Manager.at a salary of £1,000 a year. It had been made quite clear to Mr Harkins that any increases in salary would depend entirely on his showing a marked improvement in the returns from catering. These were early days, but Mr Harkins was showing every sign as being the man for whom we have been seeking.'

Unfortunately, the inability of the restaurant kitchen to serve a meal to anyone on the evening of 10 January 1967, due to the non-availability of the chef, heralded a parting of the ways for Mr Harkins. Such was the difficulty in recruiting and retaining kitchen staff, at one point in 1967 a rota of committee members was cooking the members' breakfasts.

It would not be until the close of 1967 that the linoleum of the restaurant was carpeted, at a cost of £732 and 12 shillings, thus transforming its appearance from a works canteen into something rather more welcoming. With the passage of time, various meeting rooms and lounges would be named after figures in the history of the club or significant events in British history. A description of each may be found in the annexes to this document. Edward Bridges was the son of Poet Laureate Robert Bridges, author of the poetry collection *The Testament of Beauty*. In the Great War Bridges served as adjutant of the 4th Battalion of the Oxfordshire and Buckinghamshire Light Infantry on the Western Front, where he was seriously wounded. Invalided out of the army and entered the Civil Service. In 1938 he succeeded Sir Maurice Hankey as Cabinet Secretary.

In 1946 he was appointed Permanent Secretary to HM Treasury and Head of the Home Civil Service, a position he would retain until 1956. He was the most eminent civil servant of his generation, in an age when the service was not short of talent. In 1957 he was raised to the peerage as Baron Bridges of Headley, in the County of Surrey, and of St Nicholas at Wade, in the County of Kent. He was invested a Knight of the Garter in 1965 and died in 1969. Historian Peter Hennessy in his book *Whitehall* would describe Bridges as: 'the finest flowering of the Victorian public servant - high minded, politically neutral, a gifted all-rounder who believed that government was best served by crowding the higher Civil Service with latter-day Renaissance men.' The club's Edward Bridges Room is named in his honour. More about his life may be found at Annex B.

Stuart Milner-Barry was educated at Cheltenham College and was an outstanding chess player, winning the first British Boys' Championship in 1923. He won a scholarship to Trinity College, Cambridge, taking First Class honours in Classics (part I) and Moral Sciences (part II). At the outbreak of the Second World War he was recruited to the top-secret Government Code and Cypher School at Bletchley Park, where he eventually ran Hut 6. Its task was to crack the Enigma codes used by the Wehrmacht and Luftwaffe.

After the war Milner-Barry joined HM Treasury as a principal. Apart from a stint in the Ministry of Health in the period 1958-60, he remained with the Treasury until 1966 when, aged 60, he reached retirement age. He stayed on to run the honours system. He was appointed OBE in 1946 for his work at Bletchley Park, CB in 1962 for his endeavours at HM Treasury and KCVO in 1975. Sir Stuart was one of the earliest trustees of the Civil Service Club. He finally retired in 1977 and died in 1995. The Milner-Barry Room is named in his honour. More on his remarkable life and work may be found at Annex C.

The Tea Bar on the Ground Floor in the 1960s

Of Mice and Men

The early volumes of the club's minute books explore, in some detail, the comings and goings of staff. Any number of second chefs came and went. Reliable waitresses and chambermaids could not be had for love nor money. Casual staff were heavily relied upon, with the services of Westminster Labour Exchange being in constant demand. The departure of two Chinese chefs is also explored. Upon the catering manager attempting to allocate them to different shifts, it became apparent that one of them spoke no English at all, a shortcoming that could well have been identified at the time of his recruitment.

However, the club had one weapon in its armoury which it deployed effectively. From the outset it operated a Christmas bonus scheme and the sums involved were most generous by the standards of the day. The longer a member of staff had served, the greater the bonus. This had a considerable effect on staff retention in a highly competitive labour market. Another factor in play was no doubt the solicitude of the Management Committee when it came to all matters relating to staff. Much attention was paid to provision for staff who were ill, former staff fallen on hard times, or those who had given lengthy service. Throughout 1968 bulletins on the waning health of Mrs 'Dolly' Piper, a long-serving member of staff, would regularly feature in the minutes of the Management Committee. The minutes of 7 January 1969 disclose: 'The secretary reported that since the last Management Committee meeting, news had been received that Mrs Piper had suffered another heart attack and this time it had been fatal. As her husband was still in hospital, this news had been kept from him. However, on Christmas Eve, he too expired.

In October 1966 the issue of club staff drinking whilst on duty was finally resolved, with the placing of a notice on the board in the staff rest room, that the practice was now prohibited. At the same time, the bar staff were instructed that they were not to serve any member of staff alcohol whilst they were on duty. At that point in proceedings there was not the clear distinction of roles between the management and committee members that obtains today and, consequently, some of the brighter members of staff played off the committee members against the management team by saying that the beer they were drinking had been purchased for them by such-and-such a committee member.

In February 1968 Sir William Armstrong succeeded Sir Laurence Helsby as the club's president. Sir Laurence was created a life peer on 21 May 1968, with the title Baron Helsby of Logmore, in the County of Surrey. Both Armstrong and Helsby had served together as joint permanent secretaries of HM Treasury in the years 1963-68.

One of the hazards of occupying a building next-door to a working Metropolitan Police stables is the presence of mice. On 19 November 1968 mouse droppings were discovered in the downstairs kitchen of the club and the club secretary was informed. He quickly came to the conclusion that the place was overrun by mice. On telephoning the Ministry of Works he added insistence to the matter by advising them that, unless urgent action were taken, the club would soon be moving down Whitehall, carried on the backs of mice. That same afternoon an inspection was carried out by a hygiene officer from the Ministry of Works and a rodent control officer. It soon became apparent that a large-scale infestation had taken place, as all the dressers and cupboards in the kitchen bore signs of the presence of mice. In one cupboard there was a three-and-a-half-pound tin of chocolate sauce. Embedded in its centre was a deceased rodent. The adoption of new hygiene procedures by catering staff and the laying of bait quickly resolved the problem.

More Recent Times

On the afternoon of 8 March 1973 the Irish Republican Army detonated a car bomb in the street outside the club, having first telephoned a warning to the Metropolitan Police. Their target was the army's Central London Recruiting Depot at 1-5 Great Scotland Yard.

The bomb's detonation caused chaos for the club, resulting in broken window frames, fallen ceilings and shattered glass everywhere. Fortunately, both staff and members had been evacuated. There were no casualties. Sir William Armstrong, Permanent Secretary of the Civil Service Department and Head of the Home Civil Service, visited the club later that evening and paid tribute to the efforts of all involved in restoring the premises. Dolours Price and her sister Marion were arrested at Heathrow Airport, along with Gerry Kelly, Hugh Feeney and six others, as they were boarding flights to Belfast and Dublin. They were part of an eleven-strong IRA unit, which had planted devices at the Old Bailey, Great Scotland Yard and the BBC's Armed Forces Radio Studio in Dean Stanley Street. The gang was tried in the Great Hall of Winchester Castle and convicted on 14 November 1973. The sisters would each serve 20 years in prison. A heightened security state would be an enduringly tiresome feature of life in Whitehall throughout the 1970s, 80s and 90s. On 3 February 1979 the club celebrated its Silver Jubilee, with a programme of events presided over by Chairman Maurice Mendoza.

On 1 February 1983 Ordinary Members (London) were paying a subscription of £10.00 per annum, with Country Members paying £5.00. Throughout the 1980s the club underwent a dizzying programme of redecoration and re-invention. The OK Bar would become The Buttery, and subsequently The Wine Bar. Over the following years the main bar would be moved from the ground floor to take up residence in the first-floor restaurant on no fewer than three occasions, to enable refurbishment to take place downstairs, with varying degrees of success. Throughout the 1990s and the 'noughties' the club's management expanded the activities available to members, with discos, poker, karaoke, barbeques, comedy nights, quiz nights, wine tasting, guided tours and bridge all making their appearance. On the evening of 4 February 1993 the club hosted Prime Minister John Major as principal guest at its Annual Dinner, in the company of Club President Sir Robin Butler and Sir Brian Unwin, Chairman of the CSSC. In May 2011 the CSSC closed their Chadwick Street Recreation Centre at the Horseferry Road end of the parish and the Civil Service Club happily extended a welcome to its membership.

In 2013 the club celebrated its Diamond Anniversary, with a full programme of events, presided over by long-serving Chairman John Whittaker. He passed away in 2017, within a couple of months of his Cabinet Office colleague and predecessor as club chairman, John Barker. Their many years of devoted service to the club and its members are commemorated by a brushed steel plaque affixed to the right-hand wall of the club's first floor restaurant, which reads: 'In warm appreciation and fond memory of John Barker CB and John Whittaker CBE / Honorary Officers of the Civil Service Club 2004-2017.'

So much for the Civil Service Club, a relatively recent addition to the distinguished history of Whitehall. However, the plot of land on which it stands offers an equally fascinating tale and will be of interest to the historically-minded. Along the way it touches on such diverse issues as the fall of Cardinal Thomas Wolsey, the endeavours of architect Inigo Jones, the founding of the Metropolitan Police, the labours of civil engineer Sir Joseph Bazalgette, the origins of the London Fire Brigade and the Festival of Britain.

Great Scotland Yard in the 20th Century

The Blitz comes to Great Scotland Yard in 1940.

The Afternoon of 8 March 1973.

The Priory and Hospital of St Mary Rounceval

Remarkable though it may seem to the reader, our story begins on 15 August 778 AD in a high mountain pass in the Pyrenees, near the border between France and Spain. That place being the traditional site of the Battle of Roncesvalles, in which the Basques ambushed and slaughtered the rear-guard of the Frankish army, as it was making its way across the mountains to Aquitaine in France. Charlemagne, King of the Lombards, was then campaigning in Spain. He ravaged several towns south of the Pyrenees and razed the City of Pamplona. His Frankish army was led by Seneschal Eggihard and the rear-guard by Roland, Prefect of the March of Brittany. The events of that day form the basis of the legend of the hero Roland, immortalised in the epic poem *La Chanson de Roland*, which would assume mythical dimensions in both medieval and renaissance literature.

In 1130 Sancho de la Rosa, Bishop of Pamplona, founded an Augustinian abbey at Roncesvalles for the use of pilgrims, especially those on their way to Santiago de Compostela. The monks came to England in 1199 and, in 1231, William Marshall, 2nd Earl of Pembroke founded the Priory and Hospital of St Mary Rounceval at the hamlet of Charing in Middlesex, ostensibly to aid pilgrims on their way to the shrine of Edward the Confessor at Westminster Abbey. It was a daughter house of the monastery at Roncesvalles. The community originally consisted of a prior and brethren, who were subject to the rule of the mother house. Like all medieval hospitals, St Mary Rounceval was overtly religious in nature, being run by monks and drawing its inspiration from the Corporal and Spiritual Works of Mercy of Christianity. However, a 13th century hospital bears little comparison to any modern institution bearing that title today. The best that anyone who was taken ill could expect was a bed, food and comfort in their 'hour of need'.

Medical expertise was almost non-existent, other than a knowledge of herbs and their curative properties. From descriptions given in deeds and plans, we can calculate that the priory and hospital occupied all of the land south of Charing, bounded by modern-day Whitehall, Great Scotland Yard and Northumberland Avenue. It distributed indulgences in the name of the Bishop of Pamplona and was notorious for abuses, even before the scandal of 1382 in which the brethren were found to have forged a bull of excessive indulgence. In that age, indulgences were sold by church officials for the forgiveness of sins. With a sly nod and a wink to his readers, in his book *The Canterbury Tales* (1400), Geoffrey Chaucer would write: 'With hym ther rood a gentil Pardoner, Of Rouncivale, his freend and his compeer, That streight was comen fro the court of Rome.'

Chaucer's pardoner openly admitted corruption, whilst freely hawking his wares. Such abuses were an affront to devout Christians and, in time, would lead to a German former monk named Martin Luther nailing his 95 theses to the door of All Saints' Church in Wittenberg on 31 October 1517, thereby triggering the Protestant Reformation.

In the reign of King Henry V, Rounceval was suppressed for belonging to an alien monastery, with all the other houses of that kind in the kingdom. It was restored by King Edward IV, only to be finally disbanded in King Henry VIII's Dissolution of the Monasteries. He also seized their almshouse. The chapel and its appurtenances were granted in 1605 by King Edward VI to Sir Thomas Cawarden, Master of the Revels. The chapel was demolished in 1608. Most of the hospital was removed and the land became in large part, the site on which Henry Howard would build Northampton House in 1608-09. Some of the monastic quarters remained as a private residences, until they were demolished in 1705.

Yorke Place

The Palace of Westminster dates from the early eleventh century, when King Canute built his royal residence on the north bank of the River Thames. Successive kings added to the complex. At the close of his reign, King Edward the Confessor built Westminster Abbey on Thorney Island. He breathed his last on the stormy night of 4-5 January 1066, bequeathing the English a succession crisis, which would result in the Norman Conquest.

A man of boundless energy, William the Conqueror commenced building a new palace. His short-lived son, William Rufus, continued the process, which included Westminster Hall, commenced in 1097. King Henry III set in hand the construction of new buildings for the Exchequer and the Court of Common Pleas, along with the Court of the King's Bench and the Court of Chancery. By 1245 the king's throne was situated in the palace, signifying that it was literally the seat of royal power. The old Palace of Westminster was destroyed by fire in 1512, although it retained (and still does) its status as a royal palace. Over the centuries, what was left of the palace gradually gained an accretion of new buildings, until the fire of 1834, which destroyed all of it, excepting Westminster Hall. That building, with its magnificent hammer-beam roof, the largest medieval timber roof in Northern Europe dating from 1399 is now incorporated into the replacement palace, which today serves as the United Kingdom's Houses of Parliament.

History tells us that there was a palace standing on the site of modern-day Whitehall as early as the reign of King Henry III, when Hubert de Burgh, Earl of Kent, purchased land from the monks of Westminster Abbey and resided there. He was Justiciar of England and Ireland and one of the most powerful men in the kingdom during the reigns of King John and of his infant son and successor, King Henry III.

According to the chronicler Matthew Paris, upon his death in 1243, de Burgh was buried in the Church of the Friars Preachers (commonly called the 'Black Friars') in Holborn and he left 'Yorke Place', as it was then known, to the friars. They sold it to the prelate and statesman Walter de Grey, who transferred it to the See of York as that diocese's London residence. The archbishopric would retain possession of the property for nearly three centuries. In 1514 Thomas Wolsey (created cardinal the following year) was translated from Lincoln to York. The accounts for 1514-16 'concernyng bildyngs at Yorke Place' show that 'reparacions and workemanshypp … in my lord of Yorkes Place' were being extensively carried out during those years. Among other buildings mentioned are: the hall, the chapel, 'the grete gate towards the strete,' 'the grete bakery gate into the Gardyn,' 'a breke wall from the brode gate ayenst the Grene unto the grete gatehouse of my lords place,' the chapel garden, the counting-house, the bake-house, the kitchen, the buttery, the wine-cellar, the fish-house, the scullery and the wardrobe. Despite Wolsey being the son of an Ipswich butcher, that able and ambitious prince of the church's appetite for the finer things in life would ensure Yorke Place's transformation into one of the most sumptuous residences in England, rivalled only by the Archbishop of Canterbury's Lambeth Palace. Unlike his Lord and Saviour, Cardinal Wolsey dined off the finest gold plate and King Henry VIII was well-acquainted with Yorke Place's galleries: 'hanged with cloths of gold and tissue of divers makings and cloths of silver likewise on both sides and rich cloths of baudkin of divers colours.' Notwithstanding that he was Lord Chancellor of England, one marvels at the unwisdom of the servant outshining his royal master and wonders whether he ever pondered the likely consequences of his actions.

The Palace of Whitehall

Cardinal Wolsey's inability to persuade Pope Clement VII to grant Henry an annulment of his marriage to the childless Queen Catherine of Aragon spelled his certain doom. On 19 October 1529 he was deprived of the Great Seal and informed that the king wished him to retire to Esher. On 22 October he executed a deed acknowledging that he had incurred a praemunire (a 1353 statute which forbade, on pain of outlawry, confiscation of goods and imprisonment at the king's pleasure, all appeals to authorities outside England in cases cognizable before the royal courts). He asked the king as part-recompense, to take into his hands all of his temporal possessions. He then retreated to his See to undertake those spiritual duties he had neglected during his long years in government. He was recalled to answer charges of treason - a device frequently used by Henry against those who had incurred his displeasure. Wolsey headed south for Westminster, but escaped his fate by expiring of natural causes at Leicester Abbey on 29 November 1529.

Henry had set his heart on obtaining Yorke Place, but there were difficulties, owing to the fact that it was not the cardinal's private property, belonging as it did, to the See of York. However, as Cardinal Wolsey had learned the hard way, Henry's patience was finite. Once his will was known, no man could gainsay him and expect to survive his wrath.

Although Henry had been born at the Palace of Placentia in Greenwich, as were his two daughters Mary and Elizabeth, he was determined to transform Yorke Place into his principal London residence. He embarked on the most ambitious building programme ever undertaken by an English monarch and would expend prodigious sums to realise his vision. By fair means or foul, he acquired all the land between Charing Cross and Westminster, incorporating the land from the Thames to St James's Park and Green Park.

Henry hired the Flemish artist Anton van den Wyngaerde, who laid out extensive ornamental gardens, tennis courts, a tilt-yard for jousting, a bowling alley, a cock-pit, a mews, accommodation for the court and a barracks. By the time the work was complete, the new palace covered some 23 acres and Henry had supplanted the Abbot of Westminster as the neighbourhood's principal landowner. The name 'Whitehall' or 'White Hall' is first recorded in 1532, having its origin in the Ashlar stone used for the buildings.

William Shakespeare's 1613 play *Henry VIII* contains the line: 'You must no more call it York Place - that is past: For since the Cardinal fell that title's lost; 'Tis now the King's and called Whitehall.' At that point, the thoroughfare we know today as Whitehall was called 'Kinges Streate' and it bisected the Palace of Whitehall, being a public right of way. The two halves of the palace were connected by a gatehouse, the brick-built Holbein Gate, which enabled Henry to traverse the palace unseen. He married Anne Boleyn at Whitehall in a secret ceremony on 25 January 1533 and Jane Seymour there on 30 May 1536. King Henry VIII was called to meet his maker at Whitehall on 28 January 1547.

In the early 1600s visiting Moravian nobleman Baron Wildstein would describe the palace as: 'A place that fills one with wonder ... because of the magnificence of its bedchambers and living rooms, which are furnished with the most gorgeous splendour.' The Union of the Crowns occurred with the accession of James VI, King of Scots, to the thrones of England and Ireland, which unified the realms of England, Scotland and Ireland for the first time under a single monarch on 24 March 1603. That event followed the death of Queen Elizabeth I of England – King Henry VIII's daughter, the ultimate monarch of the Tudor dynasty and James's unmarried and childless first cousin, once removed.

Scotland

The derivation of the name 'Scotland' for the northern component of the Whitehall neighbourhood may be found in the chronicler John Stow's *A Survay of London* (1598) which tells us: 'On the left hand from Charing Cross bee also divers fayre Tenements lately builded, till ye come to a large plotte of ground inclosed with bricke, and is called Scotland, where great buildings hath beene for receipt of the kings of Scotland, and other estates of that countrey; for Margaret Queene of Scots and sister to King Henry the eight, had her abiding there, when she came into England after the death of her husband, as the kings of Scotland had in former times, when they came to the Parliament of England.'

An earlier account is contained in Nicholas Bodrugan's 1548 propaganda document, entitled *An Epitome of the title that the Kynges Maiestie of Englande hath to the sovereigntie of Scotlande* printed to promote young King Edward VI's claim to the Scottish throne. The passage runs: 'This Edgar enioyned this Keneth there kyng ones in every yere, to repaire unto him into England for the makyng of lawes, which in those daies was by the noble men or piers accordyng to the order of Fraunce at this daie: to whiche ende this Edgar gave him a piece of grounde liyng beside the new palace of Westminster, upon whiche this Keneth builded a house, whiche by him and his posteritie was enioyed untill the reigne of Kyng Henry the seconde, in whose tyme upon rebellion by Willyam then kyng of Scottes, it was resumed into the kyng of Englandes handes; ye house is decayed, but the ground where it stode is called Scotland to this day.'

In 1296 King Edward I, 'Hammer of the Scots', invaded the Kingdom of Scotland in order to punish King John Balliol for his refusal to support English military action in France. Concurrently, he addressed a writ to the Sheriff of Middlesex, ordering him to seize any land or property in the county belonging either to the King of Scots or his subjects. The sheriff returned the writ endorsed with a note that: 'Neither the King of Scots nor anyone 'de regno Scocie' held property in Middlesex, except Balliol, who held the vill of Tottenham.' In 1436, in an inquisition taken before the Escheator of Middlesex, twelve jurors of Westminster stated that a piece of land, 14 perches in length along the street leading from Charing Cross to Westminster and six perches in width from the said street towards the Thames, had been given by a former king of England to a former king of Scotland, in order that the latter might build a house there in which to lodge when attending parliament but that, owing to the hostilities between the two kings, the land had not been built on. They added that a certain Richard Scarburgh received the profits of the ground, but were ignorant of his title to do so. The escheator's account for that year stated that he had taken the ground into the king's hand because of the outbreak of war with Scotland. In the following year custody of the ground was granted to John Prud and it is then described as a parcel of ground formerly belonging to the King of Scotland, lying between the 'hospicium' of the Archbishop of York on the south and the chapel of St Mary Rounceval on the north, the River of Thames on the east and the street on the west.

In November 1519 King Henry VIII granted 'Scotland' to Cardinal Wolsey as: 'a parcel of land which formerly belonged to the King of Scotland, in the County of Middlesex, with all appurtenances thereto belonging, as it lies between the inn of the Lord Archbishop of York on the south and the chapel of the Blessed Mary of Runcevall on the north and the water of Thames on the east and the royal way which leads from Charyngecrosse to Westminster on the west, now being in our hands.'

Scotland Yard

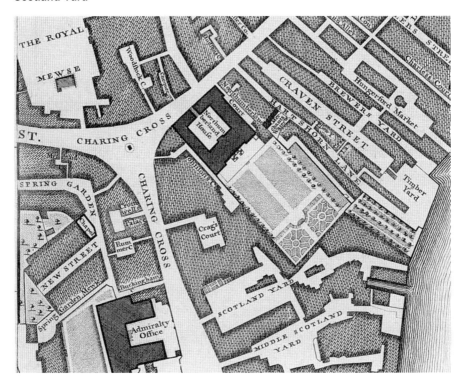

Northumberland House on John Rocque's 1746 map of London.

During the course of his programme of works which expanded Yorke Place, Cardinal Wolsey left the area then known as 'Scotland' largely untouched. During the construction of King Henry VIII's new palace, that neighbourhood increasingly came to be used by the Office of the King's Works to house its burgeoning multitude of workshops and stores. Its wharf was ideal for unloading the substantial quantities of stone, timber and materials required for the extensive building works. It also contained a guard house and a granary.

Whilst the standards of cartography in the 18th and 19th century come nowhere close to the pin-point accuracy of modern-day Ordinance Survey, what can be ascertained with a fair degree of certainty from both John Rocque's 1746 map of London and Messrs Chawner and Rhodes' meticulously hand-drawn 1829 map of Great Scotland Yard in the National Archives at Kew is that the bottom left-hand corner of the gardens of Northumberland House are the current location of the Civil Service Club at 13-15 Great Scotland Yard. In 1931 that portion of the roadway titled 'Charing Cross', which ran from Trafalgar Square down into Whitehall was incorporated into Whitehall.

The Office of the King's Works

The Office of the King's Works was established in 1378 to oversee the building and repair of the royal castles and residences. In 1832 it became the Works Department within the Office of Woods, Forests, Land Revenues, Works and Buildings. It was reconstituted as a government department in 1851 and became part of the Ministry of Works in 1940. The latter organisation would play an important role in the story of the Civil Service Club.

By the start of the 17th century Scotland housed the Office of the King's Works and began to be described in accounts and documents as 'Scotland Yard'. In 1615 Inigo Jones succeeded Simon Basil as the King's Surveyor of Works, which placed him in charge of royal architectural projects the length and breadth of the realm. Neither Basil nor his predecessors had been men of exceptional attainments, the Royal Works in Queen Elizabeth's time having been little more than a maintenance department. As one of the first Englishmen to study architecture in Italy and a devoted student of the principles of Andrea Palladio, Jones would transform that organisation into something altogether more ambitious. In his capacity as Surveyor he carried out the first proper survey of the standing stones at Stonehenge in Wiltshire. In 1619 the Banqueting House in Whitehall was destroyed by fire and, between that year and 1622, Jones replaced it with the magnificent construction that has always been regarded as his greatest achievement.

At the outbreak of the English Civil War in 1642 Jones was compelled to relinquish his office as Surveyor of Works and was with John Paulet, 5th Marquess of Winchester at the Third Siege of Basing House at Basingstoke, where, during the chaotic storming and sacking of that place, he was taken prisoner by Oliver Cromwell's men on 14 October 1645, clad only in a blanket. The marquess was discovered hiding in a bread oven.

Much of Jones' work would be destroyed in the Great Fire of London in 1666. However, enough survives to demonstrate his genius. The poet John Milton is known to have had his lodgings in Scotland Yard, whilst serving as Latin Secretary to Oliver Cromwell. By that stage the sprawling Whitehall Palace was a hotch-potch of buildings in various architectural styles, with no unifying theme. Samuel Sorbiére, French physician and translator, visited England in 1665 and described it thus: 'Ill Built, and nothing but a heap of Houses, erected at divers times, and of different Models, which they made Contiguous in the best Manner they could for the Residence of the Court; Which yet makes it a more Commodious Habitation than the Louvre, for it contains above Two Thousand Rooms, and that between a Fine Park and a Noble River so that 'tis admirably well Situated for the Conveniency of walking and going about Business into the City.' At the end of the 17th century Sorbiére's countryman, the Duc de Saint-Simon, put it rather more succinctly, describing Whitehall as: 'The largest and ugliest palace in Europe.'

On the afternoon of 4 January 1698 a Flemish laundry-maid was drying wet linen sheets on a charcoal brazier in one of the bedchambers of Whitehall Palace. It was forbidden to leave braziers unattended. However, for reasons unknown, the maid left the room. In her absence, it only took moments for the sheets to ignite and set fire to the bed hangings. In the days following, the entire, rambling Palace of Whitehall burned to the ground. An anguished King William III implored Surveyor of Works Sir Christopher Wren to save the Banqueting House. Wren instructed his bricklayers to block-up the main window on the building's south side to prevent the flames from entering. Some 20 buildings were destroyed or pulled down to create a firebreak and the building was saved.

Northumberland House

Henry Howard, the second son of Henry, Earl of Surrey was in disfavour throughout Queen Elizabeth's reign, on account of his association with Mary Queen of Scots and his Catholic sympathies. He succeeded, however, in ingratiating himself with her successor, King James VI of Scotland, upon whose accession to the English throne he was sworn of the Privy Council. He was created Earl of Northampton in 1604 and gained notoriety on account of his suspected complicity in the murder of Sir Thomas Overbury in the Tower of London, but nothing was ever proved against him. In the period 1608-09 he built a large Jacobean townhouse facing onto Charing Cross, which included extensive gardens and adjoined Scotland Yard to the west. That site was the eastern portion of the former property of the Chapel and Hospital of St Mary Rounceval. The house, which was of brick, with stone dressings, was initially designated 'Northampton House'. The façade of the building in The Strand was some 162 feet wide, the depth of the house being marginally greater. It had a single central courtyard and turrets in each corner. The layout reflected medieval tradition, with a great hall and separate apartments for members of the household. Many of the apartments were reached from external doors in the courtyard in a manner still seen at certain Oxford colleges. The exterior was embellished with classical ornament. The most striking external feature was the elaborate four-storey carved stone gateway fronting The Strand. The garden was 160 feet wide and more than 300 feet long, but, unlike its neighbours to the east, did not extend all the way down to the River Thames.

Upon Northampton's death in 1614 the property passed to his nephew, Thomas Howard, 1st Earl of Suffolk, who had commanded the GOLDEN LION in the defeat of the Spanish Armada in the action-packed summer of 1588. That property would then become known as 'Suffolk House'. Howard was appointed Lord High Treasurer in 1614, but was suspended from office in 1618 for embezzling funds. However, he retained the king's favour and the greater part of the fine imposed upon him was remitted. He died at Suffolk House in May 1626. Ownership of the house passed successively to his son Theophilus, 2nd Earl of Suffolk, who died there in June 1640 and his grandson James, the 3rd Earl.

In 1642 Lady Elizabeth Howard, second daughter of Theophilus, married Algernon Percy, 10th Earl of Northumberland and, by her marriage settlement, Suffolk House was transferred to the bridegroom upon payment of £15,000 to his wife's family. It then became known as 'Northumberland House'. It suffered damage in the John Wilkes-inspired riots of May 1768, when Hugh Percy, 1st Duke of Northumberland saved his property by the quick-thinking expedient of opening Ye Old Ship Tavern (today's Trafalgar Studios), thus distracting the mob. In the mid-19th century the grand mansions on The Strand disappeared one by one, as the area became increasingly commercial, rendering it unfashionable to the aristocracy. George Percy, 5th Duke of Northumberland was reluctant to quit his London home, but came under pressure from the Metropolitan Board of Works, which wished to build a new thoroughfare through the site. After a fire, which caused considerable damage, in 1866, he accepted an offer of £500,000 (equivalent to £58,463,157.89 in 2018). Northumberland House was demolished and Northumberland Avenue constructed in its place, connecting Trafalgar Square with Victoria Embankment. Designed by Sir Joseph Bazalgette, Chief Engineer of the Metropolitan Board of Works, the cut-and-cover tunnel for the Metropolitan District Railway would be built within the Victoria Embankment, and roofed over to take the new roadway along the River Thames.

The Evolution of Scotland Yard

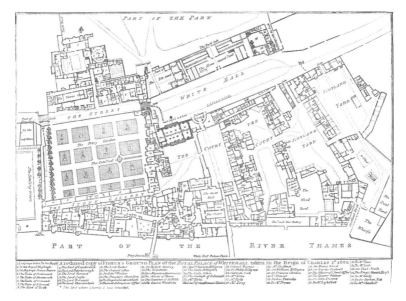

John Fisher's 1680 plan of the Palace of Whitehall.

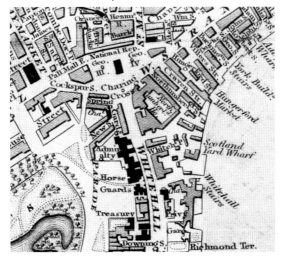

Detail of *The Improved Map of London* engraved by William Schmollinger, 1833.

Great Scotland Yard

Richard Horwood's 1799 map of London depicts Great Scotland Yard on the east side of Whitehall, opposite Thomas Ripley's Admiralty. Below it are two streets that were culs-de-sac: Middle Scotland Yard, where Whitehall Place is today, and Lower Scotland Yard, entered from Middle Scotland Yard. Lower Scotland Yard was where architect Clyde Young's neo-Baroque War Office building would be erected in 1906, but was, according to the 1862 map of the area, renamed Middle Scotland Yard when Whitehall Place, originally a cul-de-sac, took the place of the original Middle Scotland Yard.

The post of Commissioner of Police for the Metropolis was created by the Metropolitan Police Act 1829 and until 1855, was held jointly by two individuals, initially Lieutenant-Colonel Charles Rowan and barrister Richard Mayne (appointed without interview). Their office at 4 Whitehall Place had its rear entrance, used by the public, on Great Scotland Yard. That circumstance would forever link the name of the locality with the story of the Metropolitan Police, serving as its headquarters for some 60 years.

On 30 May 1884 Fenians exploded a bomb, which blew a hole in the wall of Scotland Yard and damaged the Rising Sun Public House opposite. The enterprising publican charged sightseers 3d a head to inspect the damage. In 1892 the police relocated to the turreted premises on the Victoria Embankment designed by Richard Norman Shaw which would in time, become known as 'New Scotland Yard'.

In 1967, needing a larger headquarters, a further move took place to Broadway, SW1, which would also be designated 'New Scotland Yard'. There, the headquarters remained for just under half a century, before returning in 2016 to the Thames waterfront, in the form of the redesigned Curtis Green Building on Victoria Embankment, situated between the Norman Shaw Buildings and the Ministry of Defence. Today Norman Shaw North and Norman Shaw South are part of the parliamentary estate, housing offices of members of parliament. Originally constructed for the Earl of Lonsdale and subsequently acquired by the First Lord of the Admiralty, the Metropolitan Police's Mounted Branch Stables are at 7-11 Great Scotland Yard, next-door to the club.

In 1862 civil engineer Sir Joseph Bazalgette commenced work on the construction of his Victoria Embankment to regularise the passage of the River Thames. It was but one element of a three-part work, the other parts being the Albert Embankment, from the Lambeth end of Westminster Bridge to Vauxhall; and the Chelsea Embankment, extending from Millbank to the Cadogan Pier at Chelsea. The Victoria Embankment phase was completed in July 1870. It reclaimed 22 acres of land from the river and from that point on, the Thames would no longer lap at the eastern end of Scotland Yard. Scotland Dock would be filled in and its wharf dismantled. Bazalgette not only embanked the river, but also built three bridges (Hammersmith, Putney and Battersea) across it.

By the late 19th century the layout of the neighbourhood started to resemble what we recognise today. Standing on the corner of Great Scotland Yard and Whitehall, the Clarence Public House, named after the Duke of Clarence, dates from 1896. At the time of its original construction, the design incorporated an arch across the roadway of Great Scotland Yard and it was not there for ornamental reasons, given that it supported two storeys of the pub and abutted the building alongside it in Whitehall. However, it quickly became apparent that the archway was far too narrow for the volume of traffic trying to access it. That awkward architectural feature would be removed in 1908.

Great Scotland Yard Fire House

The Royal Society for the Protection of Life from Fire was formed in 1828. It helped people escape from burning buildings by providing escape ladders. Those escapes were kept in churchyards during the day and were placed on street corners at dusk.

On 1 January 1833 ten independent fire insurance companies formed the London Fire Engine Establishment. It sought to provide the public with an effective fire service. James Braidwood of Edinburgh was appointed superintendent and he introduced a uniform which, for the first time, included personal protection from firefighting hazards. With 80 firefighters and 13 fire stations, that organisation was a private enterprise funded by the insurance companies. It was primarily responsible for saving material goods from fire. Several large fires, most notably at the Palace of Westminster in October 1834 and the Great Tooley Street Fire of June 1861 (in which, Braidwood was killed), spurred the insurance companies to lobby the government to provide a fire brigade at public expense.

After due consideration, in 1865 the Metropolitan Fire Brigade Act was passed. It ordered that the Metropolitan Fire Brigade be brought into being as a public service on 1 January 1866 and charged it with the 'Protection of Life and Property from Fire within the Metropolis.' Its first leader was Superintendent Eyre Massey Shaw, a former head of police and fire services in Belfast. On 15 August 1904 that organisation was re-named the London Fire Brigade by virtue of Section 46 of the London County Council (General Powers) Act. In Norman Seymour's *The Story of 13-15 Great Scotland Yard* he related: 'On 7 October 1880, the Chief Fire Officer reported that the existing fire house in Chandos Street was no longer adequate for its task and that it could not be adapted suitably.'

The Metropolitan Board of Works searched for a site and on 14 February 1881 approved the building of a new fire house on a plot of land, in the corner of the one-time garden of Northumberland House, bounded on the Whitehall side by the Rising Sun Public House at 11 (demolished 1910) and on the Northumberland Avenue side by the Society for Promoting Christian Knowledge (today, the Nigerian High Commission).

The fire house opened in 1884 and, in large part, its layout dictates the design of today's Civil Service Club. It was designed to accommodate a married officer, 15 married men, six single men, one coachman, three engines, three escapes, one hose cart and two pairs of horses. The ground floor comprised the engine room, watch room, stables and ancillary areas. An entrance for escapes was located to the east side of the building. The original basement contained both coal and wood stores. The upper floors contained the mess, along with the single and mixed living accommodation. The building was constructed of load-bearing brickwork, comprising grey stocks laid in English bond, with red Fareham facings on the front elevation, relieved with red Mansfield stone and blue Staffordshire bricks. The building is set back 26 feet from the roadway, due to a last-minute objection from Messrs Cluttons, a firm of solicitors, which then occupied offices on the opposite side of the street. They claimed 'ancient lights'. Therefore, the yard that should have occupied the rear of the building would appear at the front instead. The fireman's watch-tower on the far left-hand side of the building can be observed by standing in the street, under the archway of Scotland Place, opposite the premises. It survives at the insistence of Westminster City Council. The introduction of the telegraph would render the tower redundant and the internal combustion engine would do the same for the horses. In 1921 the firemen would be re-located to 72 Shaftesbury Avenue

The Festival of Britain

The Ministry of Works then allocated the fire house to the Ministry of Pensions as office accommodation. That department was created in 1916 to handle the payment of war pensions. In 1939 it was expanded at the beginning of the Second World War by the secondment of civil servants from the Inland Revenue and other departments. In 1940 the entire ministry was relocated to Thornton-Cleveleys in Lancashire. During the war 13-15 Great Scotland Yard functioned as an intelligence and interrogation centre.

The notion for holding an exhibition in 1951 came from the Royal Society of Arts in 1943, believing that an international event should be held to mark the centenary of the 1851 Great Exhibition. In 1945 the government appointed a committee under Lord Ramsden to consider how exhibitions could promote exports. When it reported back, the idea of an international exhibition had been dropped on the grounds of cost and instead a series of displays about the arts, architecture, science, technology and industrial design was suggested. Clement Attlee's government seized the notion as an opportunity to give the nation a boost after the war and a chance to celebrate 'the arts of peace'. It was intended to demonstrate Britain's contribution to civilisation, past, present and future in the arts, science, technology and industrial design. The main exhibition site was on London's South Bank. That small 27-acre site had previously accommodated warehouses and a brewery damaged in The Blitz. Hugh Casson was appointed Director of Architecture for the Festival and he brought in dozens of young architects to design the site's buildings and landscaping. On 3 May 1951 King George VI opened the Royal Festival Hall on London's South Bank. Gerald Barry, the Festival Director summed up the hopes of the organisers by describing it as a: 'tonic to the nation'. Although the main venue was in London, it was a nationwide affair, with exhibitions in many towns and cities throughout Britain. Events included the London South Bank Exhibition with its futuristic-looking Dome of Discovery, which was then the largest aluminium structure ever to have been erected.

Another iconic structure, and the most remembered, was the Skylon. That steel and aluminium structure lacked a practical function save as a landmark and was described as '…a huge, lively joke, a tribute only to the spirit of nonsense and creative laughter'. Other sites included the Pleasure Gardens in Battersea Park and a 'Live Architecture' exhibit in Poplar, East London set out as a model for Britain's New Towns. An Exhibition of Farm and Factory was held in Belfast. Glasgow was the site of an Exhibition of Heavy Industry and two travelling exhibitions carried the Festival further afield, one aboard the decommissioned aircraft carrier HMS CAMPANIA, the other on a fleet of lorries. Hundreds of events were held up and down the country. The Festival turned a profit and was the catalyst for a new design aesthetic, launching the career of a number of textile, furniture and graphic designers. By the time the Festival closed in September 1951, more than one in three Britons had attended, over eight million at the South Bank alone. Today, the only remaining element is the Royal Festival Hall, which is now a Grade I listed building, the first post-war building to become so protected. Designed by Sir Robert Matthew, Leslie Martin and Sir Hubert Bennett, it was built specifically for the project. The Festival of Britain was formally established by HM Treasury in March 1948 and existed as a separate government department from April 1949 to March 1953. At that time 13-15 Great Scotland Yard housed a press bureau, run by Bernhard 'Bert' Garai's Keystone Press Agency, which handled much of the Festival's public relations.

The Civil Service Club in 2019

ANNEX A

CIVIL SERVICE CLUB TO BE OPENED WITH THE
AID OF THE QUEEN'S WEDDING PRESENT FUND

Members of the Civil Service and Foreign Service who contributed to the Wedding Present for Her Majesty The Queen in 1947 will remember that two silver salvers were, as a token of their great regard, presented to Her Majesty. The remainder of the sum subscribed was, by her wish, to be applied to some object of general benefit to the Civil and Foreign Services.

Much time and thought has been given to devising a scheme from which industrial and non-industrial grades alike could benefit. I am now able to report that a suitable project has been evolved which has Her Majesty's warm approval. It has also been welcomed by representatives of the staff – industrial and non-industrial – who have been consulted throughout.

A Civil Service Club situated in the heart of London has long been an objective of the Civil Service Sports Council but has been unattainable for lack of funds to meet the capital expenditure involved. Her Majesty has most graciously agreed that the Fund which was subscribed for her Wedding Present should be used to enable the Council to realise this ambition. It is therefore to be handed over to the Sports Council to meet the capital expenditure required to adapt, equip and redecorate the excellent premises which the Sports Council have found, after much search. Members' subscriptions and the proceeds of charges for club services will provide the necessary annual revenue. The club premises are in Great Scotland Yard (two minutes from Trafalgar Square and Charing Cross). They could not be better placed for London civil servants as a whole, nor for their colleagues outside London, who we hope will be glad to take advantage of the amenities of the club when visiting London.

The premises will be taken over on 1 February next. For the time being the club will have the use of the three lower floors only, but it is intended to provide as soon as possible a small number of bedrooms for visiting members. In the meantime, in addition to providing a first class venue for the membership, amenities will include a full restaurant service, lounges and rooms for reading, writing, cards, television and so on.

Membership is to be open to all civil servants, industrial and non-industrial, and with a view to attracting every grade the annual subscription has been fixed at 10s. for London members and 5s. for country members.

This is an enterprise which deserves full support. The fact that Her Majesty has so generously allowed her Wedding Gift to be associated with it will, I am sure, bring a universal welcome to the club throughout the Civil and Foreign Services. Forms of application for membership will be available shortly.

EDWARD BRIDGES

11th December 1952

ANNEX B
THE BRIDGES ROOM

Edward Ettingdene Bridges was born on 4 August 1892 at Yattendon Manor in Berkshire. He was the third of the three children and only son of Robert Seymour Bridges (later Poet Laureate) and Mary Monica Waterhouse. Edward arrived at Eton in 1906, where he received a sound grounding in the Classics. He won a history demyship to Magdalen College, Oxford and went up in 1911. There he commenced reading Greats, with the object of taking his degree in two-and-a-half years, then going on to read modern history.

He was awarded a First in Greats in July 1914 but, owing to the outbreak of war in August, never got to read history. In September 1914, as an officer cadet, Bridges was called up to serve in the 4th Battalion of the Oxfordshire and Buckinghamshire Light Infantry. He saw active service in France. In 1917, Captain Bridges was seriously injured by a bullet, which shattered his right arm. He was awarded the Military Cross. Declared unfit for further service, he obtained a post as a temporary administrative assistant with HM Treasury in Whitehall. He showed such promise that Controller of Establishments Sir Malcolm Ramsay would write to the Civil Service Commissioners, recommending his assignment to HM Treasury as an assistant principal. In 1919-20 he took the All Souls Prize Fellowship Examination, which led to the award of an All Souls Fellowship. In June 1922 Bridges married Katharine Dianthe Farrer, daughter of Thomas Cecil Farrer, 2nd Baron Farrer. Their happy union was blessed with two sons and two daughters.

In the years 1927-34, Bridges was deputy establishment officer of HM Treasury and served as secretary to a number of committees, including three royal commissions. From 1926 he was Official Side Secretary to the National Whitley Council. He was promoted principal assistant secretary in January 1937 and, when Sir Maurice Hankey retired in 1938, Sir Warren Fisher, then Head of the Home Civil Service, recommended him as Secretary to the Cabinet. In that role, Sir Edward served Prime Ministers Neville Chamberlain and Winston Churchill during the darkest days of the Second World War.

Bridges was responsible for recording the decisions of the War Cabinet and its committees and ensuring that the outcome of their deliberations was put into effect. Churchill asked him for advice on how a central statistical office could be created within the prime minister's office, in order to consolidate and issue authoritative working statistics. Sir Edward's work on the subject led to the creation of the Central Statistical Office in 1941, for the purpose of handling the statistics required for the war effort and developing national income accounts. In 1946 Bridges was appointed Permanent Secretary to HM Treasury and Head of the Home Civil Service, a position he held until 1956. In 1950, he delivered a lecture, which provided an overview of the stages through which the Home Civil Service had evolved since the publication of Stafford Northcote's and Charles Trevelyan's seminal report of 1854 and would later be published as *Portrait of a Profession: The Civil Service Tradition*. In 1939, Bridges was appointed to the Order of the Bath as a Knight Commander. He was sworn of the Privy Council in 1953 and, in 1957, was raised to the peerage as Baron Bridges of Headley, in the County of Surrey and of Saint Nicholas at Wade, in the County of Kent. In 1965 he was invested a Knight of the Garter. In retirement Lord Bridges served as Chancellor of the University of Reading. He was granted honorary degrees from several universities and appointed FRS. Lord Bridges died at Winterfold Heath, Surrey on 27 August 1969 at the age of 77.

ANNEX C
THE MILNER-BARRY ROOM

Philip Stuart Milner-Barry was born on 20 September 1906 at Hendon. He was the second youngest of the five sons and daughter of teacher Edward Leopold Milner-Barry and his wife, Edith Mary Besant. Philip was educated at Cheltenham College and Trinity College, Cambridge. At the start of the Great Depression he commenced work as a stockbroker, an occupation wholly unsuited to his talents. He survived the experience through his devotion to chess. One of the most gifted attacking players of his generation, he won the British Boys' Championship in 1923 and played for England in the International Chess Olympiads of 1937, 1939, 1952, and 1956. He was chess correspondent for *The Times* 1938-45. He was playing chess for England in Argentina when war broke out in 1939.

Gordon Welchman, who had been at Trinity with Milner-Barry, recruited him to the Government Code and Cypher School (GCCS) at Bletchley Park. He joined Hut 6, which focussed on Wehrmacht and Luftwaffe Enigma signal traffic. Despite his first-class brain, Milner-Barry always maintained that he was not clever enough to be a cryptanalyst.

Initially he searched for 'cribs' (plain text of messages enciphered on Enigma), without which, it was almost impossible to break Enigma keys quickly. Bypassing Bletchley Park's leadership, Milner-Barry was joint-author with Hugh Alexander, Alan Turing and Welchman of a memorandum to Prime Minister Winston Churchill in October 1941, which explained that the lack of a small number of junior staff (probably about a hundred) was impeding the work of Huts 6 and 8 (Naval Enigma). Stewart Menzies, the head of MI6, who had overall responsibility for GCCS had neglected to ensure that it was adequately staffed. Judging himself the most expendable member of the team, Milner-Barry took the memo to the prime minister. An avid consumer of their product, Churchill swung into 'Action This Day' mode and thundered to his aide, General 'Pug' Ismay: 'Make sure they have all they want on extreme priority and report to me that this has been done.'

As Hut 6 expanded, Milner-Barry became deputy head and then head of the cryptanalytical operational watch. After the BRUSA (Britain-United States of America) agreement of May 1943 on dividing signals intelligence work against Germany, Italy and Japan, the Americans arrived in numbers. They made a highly effective contribution to the work of the team. By September 1943, when Milner-Barry became head of Hut 6, it comprised some 450 staff. He always felt that his team's grip on Enigma was precarious, but it would be sustained until the end of the war. He later wrote: 'For both Hugh and myself it was rather like playing a tournament game (sometimes several games) every day for five and a half years.' After the war, Milner-Barry joined HM Treasury as a principal. He married Thelma Tennant Wells in 1947. Under the rules of the day, she had to resign from the Treasury. They had a son and two daughters. He rose to the post of under-secretary and reached retirement age at 60 in 1966. That year Milner-Barry was appointed Civil Service Department Ceremonial Officer, with responsibility for the honours system. He finally retired in 1977. Unable to disclose his wartime role in his lifetime, it was only in the 1980s that books began to be published, explaining the crucial role played by GCCS in securing victory in the Second World War. In October 1991, Milner-Barry returned to Downing Street with a petition signed by more than 10,000 people, asking for Bletchley Park to be preserved as a monument. He was appointed OBE for his wartime work in 1946, CB in 1962 and KCVO in 1975. Sir Stuart died on 25 March 1995.

THE ELIZABETHAN ROOM

The Elizabethan Room is named after the reign (1558-1603) of England's last Tudor monarch, Queen Elizabeth I. The daughter of King Henry VIII and his second wife, Anne Boleyn, she was England's 'Gloriana' – a virgin queen, who saw herself as wedded to her country. Henry VIII's break with Rome in 1533 ushered in an era of religious division in the British Isles, although Henry's daughter Queen Mary I was Catholic and sought to re-impose Catholicism during her short reign (1552-58). Following Mary's death, Queen Elizabeth I pursued Henry's policy of rejecting papal authority, aiming to return England to the Protestant faith. As a result, England's Catholics were persecuted, the mass was banned and priests were hunted down. Elizabeth herself did not care overmuch for matters of conscience, famously stating: 'I would not open windows into men's souls.'

Under Elizabeth, England experienced domestic peace and growing prosperity. That happy circumstance in turn, fostered the flowering of cultural growth on a scale never before seen in these islands. Elizabeth's reign would usher in poets like Edmund Spenser and men of science and letters like Francis Bacon. In 1576, the actor and impresario James Burbage built The Theatre at Shoreditch, the first permanent, dedicated theatre built in England since Roman times, and it would be followed by many others. The theatre scene, which performed both for the court and nobility in private and the public in theatres, became the most crowded in Europe and summoned forth a host of playwrights, including such stellar talents as Christopher Marlowe, William Shakespeare and Ben Jonson.

Many of the writers, thinkers and artists of the day enjoyed the patronage of members of Elizabeth's court and their works often referenced the queen. These cultural achievements did not just happen to be created while Elizabeth was on the throne - rather, Elizabeth's actions, her image and the court atmosphere nurtured, influenced - even inspired - works of literature. Poetry, music, the fine arts and learning in general would all flourish. The Elizabethan Age is considered by some historians to be a 'golden age' and is so regarded, because of its contrast with the turmoil of the periods before and after it.

It brought a welcome respite between the English Reformation, with its battles between Catholics and Protestants, and the bloody contest between parliament and King Charles I, that would wrack the entire British Isles barely 30 years after Elizabeth's death.

Elizabeth made building up England's naval strength a priority. She risked war with Spain by supporting the 'Sea Dogs' John Hawkins and Francis Drake, who preyed on the Spanish merchant ships carrying gold and silver from the New World. That led to the Anglo-Spanish War of 1585-1604. When Spain finally set about invading and conquering England in 1588, that enterprise was a fiasco. Superior English ships and seamanship foiled the invasion and led to the destruction of the Spanish Armada, marking the high point of Elizabeth's reign. In her speech to the troops gathered at Tilbury Camp she told them: 'I know I have the body of a weak, feeble woman; but I have the heart and stomach of a king, and of a king of England too.' During her reign English explorers sought new trade routes and tried to expand British trade into the Spanish colonies in the Americas. Sir Francis Drake, one of the commanders in the defeat of the Armada, was one of the founders of England's naval tradition. His ship, the GOLDEN HIND was one of the first to circumnavigate the world. Sir Humphrey Gilbert taking possession of St John's in Newfoundland on 5 August 1583 signalled the foundation of Britain's overseas empire.

ANNEX E

THE TRAFALGAR ROOM

The Civil Service Club is located a mere five minutes away from Trafalgar Square, which commemorates Britain's greatest naval victory. In 1805 the First French Empire, under Napoleon Bonaparte, was the dominant military land power on the European continent, while the Royal Navy controlled the seas. Early in 1805 Vice-Admiral Lord Nelson commanded the British fleet blockading Toulon. The French fleet, under Vice-Admiral Pierre-Charles Villeneuve, evaded Nelson when the British were blown off station by storms. Nelson chased the French fleet to the Caribbean and back. At 0600 on 21 October 1805 the two fleets sighted each other off Cape Trafalgar, between Cadiz and the Strait of Gibraltar, and at 0640 Nelson gave the order 'prepare for battle'. The British fleet of 27 ships was outnumbered, the Franco-Spanish fleet of 33 vessels totalled nearly 30,000 men and 2,632 guns to Nelson's 18,000 men and 2,148 guns.

Nelson devised an unorthodox battle plan which called for his ships to attack the enemy broadside in two parallel lines, break into the enemy's formation and blast his opponents to smithereens, at close quarters. At 1150 Nelson in his flagship, HMS VICTORY, famously signalled the fleet: 'England expects that every man will do his duty.'

Villeneuve hoisted the signal 'engage the enemy' and the French vessel FOUGUEUX fired the first shots at Vice-Admiral Cuthbert Collingwood's ship ROYAL SOVEREIGN. Then Nelson's squadron, with twelve ships, attacked the van and centre of Villeneuve's line, which included Villeneuve in the BUCENTAURE. The majority of Nelson's squadron broke through and shattered Villeneuve's line in the melée. The battle progressed largely according to Nelson's plan. Six of the leading French and Spanish ships, under Rear-Admiral Pierre Dumanoir le Pelley, were ignored in the first attack and about 1530 were able to turn about to aid those behind. But Dumanoir's counter-attack failed and was driven off. Collingwood, in the ROYAL SOVEREIGN, completed the destruction of the enemy rear and the battle ended at about 1700. Nelson was mortally wounded by a sniper in the tops of the French ship REDOUBTABLE and taken below to the ship's cockpit. Captain Thomas Hardy reported to Nelson that the battle was won. 'Thank God I have done my duty' were his last words and he expired at 1630. Villeneuve was captured and his fleet lost some 14,000 men, of whom half were taken prisoners of war. His flagship BUCENTAURE was captured, along with many others. Of the 33 French and Spanish ships which departed Cadiz, only eleven would return to port. Many were wrecked in a storm as they tried to make safe harbour. Villeneuve lived to return to France, only to be murdered by Napoleon. The British, despite losing 500 sailors during the engagement, did not lose a single ship. Commissioned for service in the American War of Independence, between 1778 and 1812, HMS VICTORY took part in five naval battles. Trafalgar was not only the most famous, but also her last.

Today the oldest commissioned warship in the world may be seen at No 1 Dock in Portsmouth Historic Dockyard. On 9 January 1806 Nelson was interred with much ceremony in the crypt of St Paul's Cathedral. He was entombed in a black marble sarcophagus originally intended for Cardinal Thomas Wolsey. The Battle of Trafalgar would establish Britain as the world's dominant naval power for the next century. It also confirmed Nelson's reputation as one of the greatest military strategists of all time. To this day the Senior Service celebrates Trafalgar Day each year on its anniversary.

ANNEX F

THE CHURCHILL ROOM

Winston Churchill was born on 30 November 1874 at Blenheim Palace in Oxfordshire. His father was Lord Randolph Churchill and his mother Jennie Jerome was American. Winston attended Harrow and then Sandhurst. In 1899 he resigned from the army and travelled to South Africa to report on the Boer War. He was captured and interned, but escaped, becoming a national hero. In 1900 he was elected Conservative MP for Oldham but, after policy disagreements, crossed the floor to join the Liberals in 1904. In 1906 he became Under-Secretary of State for the Colonies. In 1908 he became MP for Dundee and that year, was appointed President of the Board of Trade. He was responsible for the Trade Boards Act of 1909, which set minimum wages for workers in certain trades.

He also introduced labour exchanges. In 1910 Churchill became Home Secretary and, in 1911, First Lord of the Admiralty. In the Great War Churchill was blamed for the failure of the Dardanelles Campaign. In July 1917 he became Minister of Munitions. The war ended in November 1918 and the Liberals won the snap election that December. In 1919 Churchill became Secretary of State for War. In 1921 he was made Secretary of State for the Colonies. In 1924 he became Chancellor of the Exchequer and, in 1925, returned the country to the gold standard, a decision he later regarded a serious mistake as it meant the pound was overvalued. He re-joined the Conservatives in 1925. In 1929 the Tories lost their majority in the Commons and a minority Labour government took office. In 1931 a national government, made up of all parties, was formed to deal with the economic crisis, but Churchill was left out in the cold. In the 1930s he argued strongly for rearmament. He opposed Prime Minister Neville Chamberlain's appeasement policy and was proved right when Germany occupied Czechoslovakia in 1939. When the Second World War began, Churchill returned to the Admiralty. Chamberlain resigned in the aftermath of the Norway Campaign and Churchill became premier on 10 May 1940.

That same day, German forces invaded Belgium and The Netherlands. France surrendered on 21 May, but the Germans lost the Battle of Britain fought in the skies over England that summer. Nevertheless, the Germans had further successes. In April 1941 they conquered Yugoslavia and Greece. In May 1941 they captured Crete. The situation began to change in June 1941, when Hitler invaded Russia. Churchill always detested communism, but promised the Russians material assistance. On 7 December 1941 the Japanese attacked Pearl Harbor. In November 1942 the British won a decisive victory at El Alamein in Egypt and, in early 1943, the Russians won a victory at Stalingrad. The Allies invaded Sicily in July 1943, then Italy in September. Meanwhile, the Russians won another victory at Kursk in July 1943 and the tide turned against the Germans. The Allies invaded France in June 1944 and Germany surrendered in May 1945. In July 1945 Labour won a general election and Churchill became Leader of the Opposition. In March 1946 with the onset of the Cold War, he gave a speech at Fulton, Missouri in which he said: 'From Stettin in the Baltic to Trieste in the Adriatic, an iron curtain has descended across the continent'. The Tories won the election in 1951 and Churchill became prime minister again. In recognition of his historical works he was awarded the Nobel Prize for Literature in 1953. He remained in office until 1955, when he resigned. He remained an MP until 1964. In the early 1960s Churchill suffered a series of strokes and died on 24 January 1965 at the age of 90. His state funeral palpably marked the end of an epoch.

ANNEX G

CHAIRMEN OF THE CIVIL SERVICE CLUB, GREAT SCOTLAND YARD

Mr F A Hartman 1953-58

Sir Frederick Aldridge 1958-1965

Mr H Pitchforth 1965-68

Anthony Sutherland 1968-73

John Perrin 1973-76

Maurice Mendoza 1976-81

Don Bryars 1981-85

Alan Atherton 1985-89

John Pestell 1989-90

Barry Miller 1990-95

David Butler 1995-97

Don Brereton 1997-2005

John Barker 2005-08

John Whittaker 2008-17

Sir Peter Housden 2017-